The best surfer out there is
the one having the most fun.

Phil Edwards

If in doubt, paddle out.

Nat Young

If you're having a bad
day, catch a wave.

Frosty Hesson

If there was no such thing as barrels I probably wouldn't even surf.

Clay Marzo

I surf to get a tan.
Shane Dorian

I'm just a surfer who wanted to build something that would allow me to surf longer.

Jack O'Neill

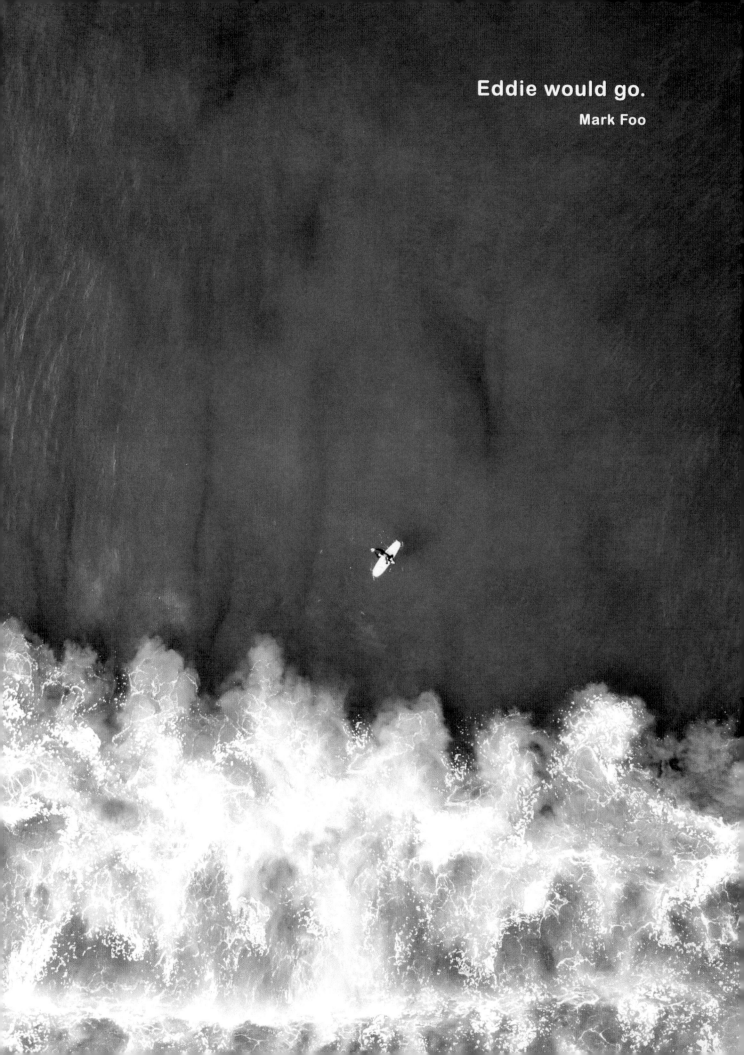

Eddie would go.
Mark Foo

Never drive away from good surf.

Roger Sharp

One drop in is an accident, two is rude, three is a twatable offence.

Roger Sharp

Sometimes in the morning, when it's a good surf, I go out there, and I don't feel like it's a bad world.

Kary Mullis

Your surfing can get better on every turn, on every wave you catch. Learn to read the ocean better. A big part of my success has been wave knowledge.

Kelly Slater

It's a culmination of your life of surfing when you turn and paddle in at Mavericks.

Jeff Clark

Big waves aren't measured in feet, but in increments of fear.

Buzzy Trent

Then, after I've gotten rid of Batman and Robin for good, I will rule the waves. Me, the Joker, king of the surf and all the surfers. Then, Gotham City! Later, the world!

The Joker

Surfing's the source.
Can change your life.
Swear to God.

Bohdi

Wiping out is an under
appreciated skill.
Laird Hamilton

Honest to goodness it's
the absolute ultimate!
Gidget

I took off on a wave, went down the side, popped out the other end, and went, shit, I'm still alive!

Greg Noll

The sea lives in every one of us.

Robert Wyland

I could not help concluding this man had the most supreme pleasure while he was driven so fast and so smoothly by the sea.

Captain James Cook

There are a million ways to surf, and as long as you're smiling you're doing it right.

Unknown

Waves are toys from God.

Clay Marzo

When the surfs up, your life is too.
Wilhelm Sverdvik

It's a cakewalk, when you know how.

Gerry Lopez

I've tried body surfing. It's nice.

Ziggy Marley

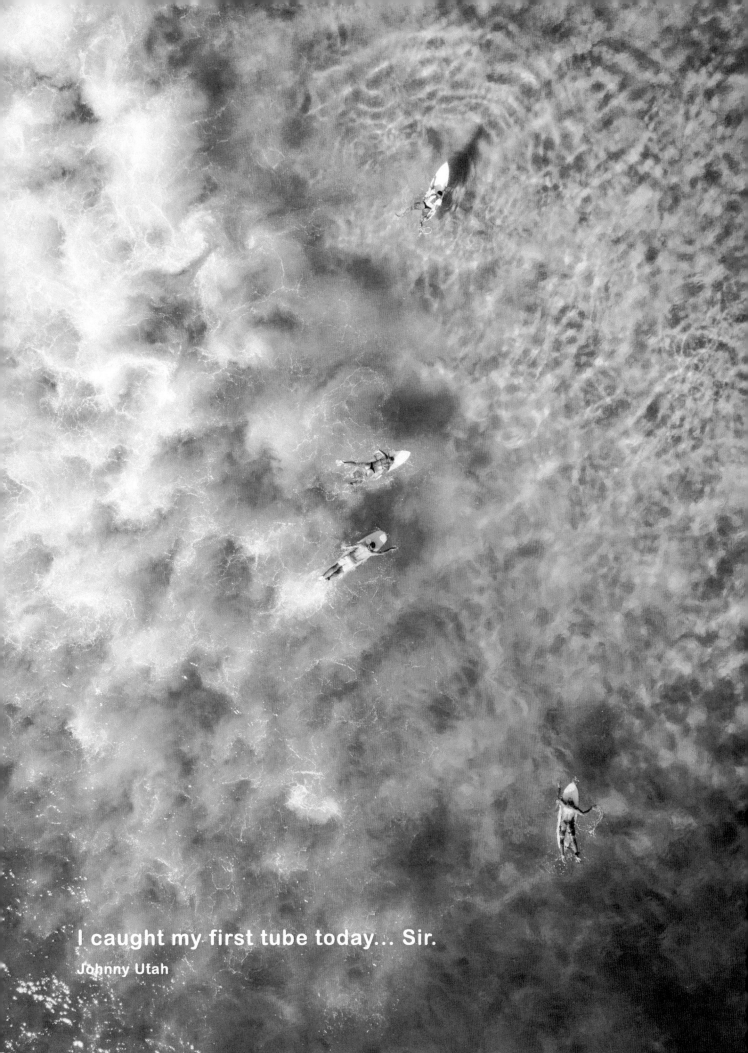

I caught my first tube today... Sir.

Johnny Utah

Go strip off your clothes that are a nuisance in this mellow clime. Get in and wrestle with the sea; wing your heels with the skill and power that reside in you, hit the sea's breakers, master them, and ride upon their backs as a king should.

Jack London

It's funny, 'cause you think surfing is your whole life, but then when you make a family it seems like it's not at all.

Joel Parkinson

The only one whom can whisper to you the ways of the surf, is the wind.

Wilhelm Sverdvik

As for my own surfing, let's just say that when the waves start pushing 10 feet, I get this tremendous urge to make a sandwich.

Bruce Jenkins

Sliding a wave removes our brains out of the ordinary and slips us into the extra ordinary of being there now. No more worries about mortgages or strife of being poor or rich. When you enter the domain of an ocean cylinder, that moment, those split seconds belong to the Zen part of just being. Period.

Bill Hamilton

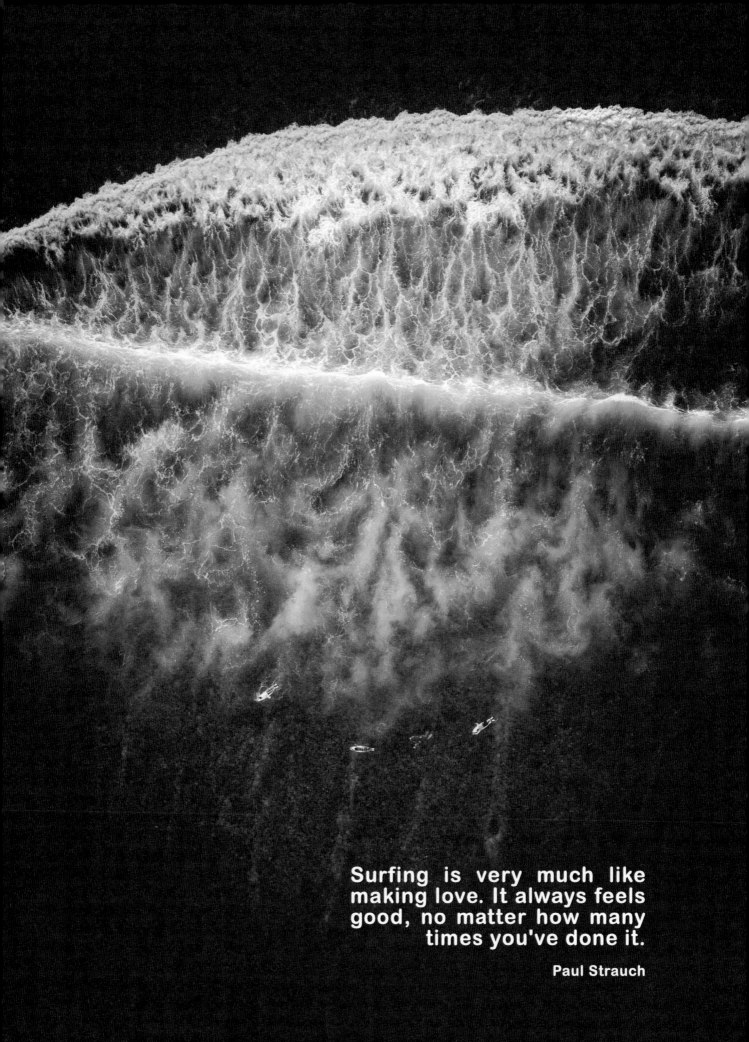

Surfing is very much like making love. It always feels good, no matter how many times you've done it.

Paul Strauch

A big wave is like a beautiful woman, exciting to look at and thrilling to ride.

Buzzy Trent

Surfing, alone among sports, generates laughter at its very suggestion, and this is because it turns not a skill into an art, but an inexplicable and useless urge into a vital way of life.

Matt Warshaw

100% pure adrenaline!

Bodhi

Live to surf, surf to live.
Mike Doyle

The best surfer out there is the one having the most fun.

Phil Edwards

Tell the teacher we're surfin'.
The Beach Boys

You will love the ocean. It makes you feel small, but not in a bad way. Small because you realize you're part of something bigger.

Lauren Myracle

I wanted freedom, open air and adventure. I found it on the sea.

Alain Gerbeault

There is not one right way to ride a wave.

Jamie O'Brien

Out of the water, I am nothing.
Duke Kahanamoku

**Surfing in crowds is like mind over matter.
If I don't mind it don't matter.**
Brodus Rogers

You're sayin' the FBI's gonna pay me to
learn to surf?

Johnny Utah

What I love the most about surfing is that it's my first love. It's the first thing I can remember being consumed by.

Stephanie Gilmore

Surfing is the most blissful experience you
can have on this planet, a taste of heaven.

John McCarthy

My passion for surfing was more than my fear of sharks.

Bethany Hamilton

There is nothing, nothing, more sad than a surfer who used to surf.

Unknown

Surfing is attitude dancing.

Gerry Lopez

we're all equal before a wave.
Laird Hamilton

Surfing soothes me, it's always been a kind of Zen experience for me. The ocean is so magnificent, peaceful, and awesome. The rest of the world disappears for me when I'm on a wave.

Paul Walker

You can't stop the waves,
but you can learn to surf.

John Kabat-Zinn

It's not tragic to die doing something you love.

Mark Foo

Why do we love the sea? It is because it has some potent power to make us think things we like to think.

Robert Henri

I think when a surfer becomes a surfer, it's almost like an obligation to be an environmentalist at the same time.

Kelly Slater

Together we can face challenges as deep as the ocean and as high as the sky.

Sonia Gandhi

The joy of surfing is so many things combined, from the physical exertion of it, to the challenge of it, to the mental side of the sport.

Kelly Slater

Dance with the waves, move with the sea, let the rhythm of the water set your soul free.

Christy Ann Martine

Surfing's one of the few
sports that you look ahead
to see what's behind.

Laird Hamilton

Surfing for me is more than
my lifestyle; it's my passion,
my love, and it's a part of me.

Bethany Hamilton

If it swells, ride it!

Unknown

It's like the mafia. Once you're in - your in. There's no getting out.

Kelly Slater

The sea does not like to be restrained.

Rick Riordan

There's nothing more beautiful than the way the ocean refuses to stop kissing the shoreline, no matter how many times it's sent away.

Sarah Kay

The ocean stirs the heart, inspires the imagination and brings eternal joy to the soul.

Robert Wylan

Surfing is attitude dancing.

Gerry Lopez

The sea has boundless patience.
Craig Robertson

**The sea will grant each man new hope,
and sleep will bring dreams of home...**

Christopher Columbus

The sea, once it casts its spell, holds one in its net of wonder forever.

Jacques Cousteau

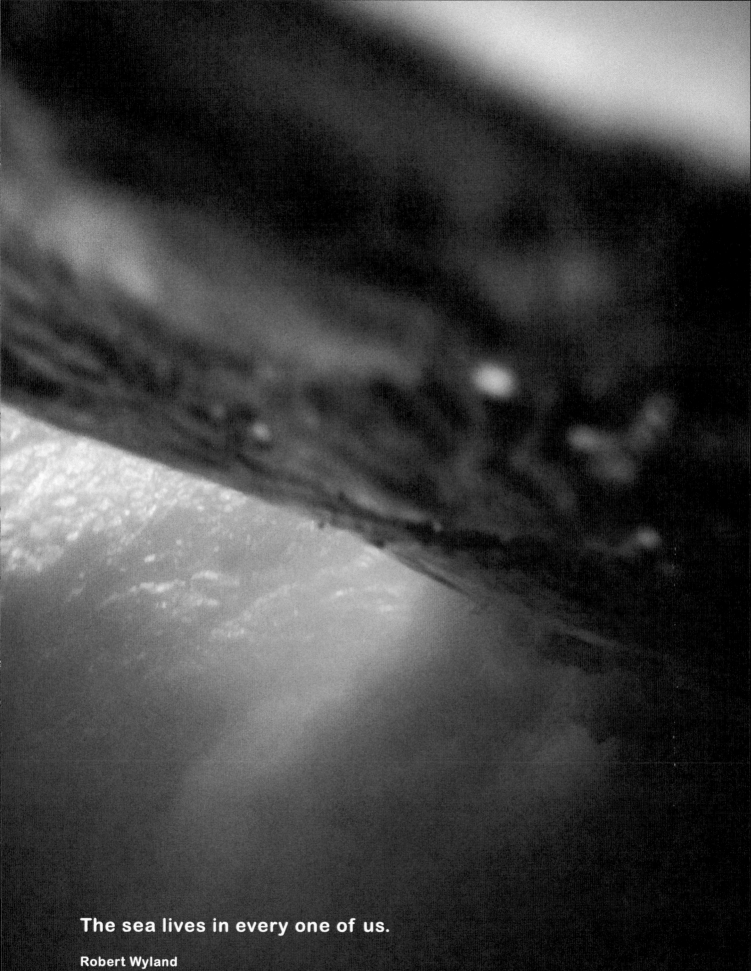

The sea lives in every one of us.

Robert Wyland

Happiness is a day at the beach.

Unknown

The waves of the sea
help me get back to me.
Unknown

Sky above, sand below, peace within.
Unknown